The Dirty Thirty

Words Even Smart People Misuse

Simple
Simplistic

Regime
Regimen

Delete

Capital
Capitol

Stationery
Stationary

**David Hatcher
and Lane Goddard**

LandaBooks
1873 Meadowbrook Drive
Winston-Salem, North Carolina 27104

www.LandaBooks.com
info@LandaBooks.com

Cover design by Paige Powell, Alexandria, Virginia
www.artbypaige.com

Printed by Lightning Source, Inc.

Contents

Introduction

We're Judged by Our Words

People judge us by our words — the ones we use, and the ones we *misuse*. Some words are misused much more often than others, and the words in this book are among the biggest troublemakers, even for good speakers and writers.

Why Are They So Hard?

One reason is that they often come in look-alike pairs, such as *affect-effect, who-whom,* and *regime-regimen.* And sometimes they're related in meaning, like *imply-infer,* and *emigrate-immigrate.* So it's easy to choose the wrong one of these near-identical twins. And because both are valid words, our spellcheckers won't give us much help in sorting them out. Fortunately, there are some simple tricks to help keep them straight.

Stalactites? Or Stalagmites?

One useful aid is mnemonics — memory hooks. As an example, let's take a pair of words that are easy to mix up: *stalactite* and *stalagmite.* They're not included in the dirty thirty, because they're not common in everyday speech. But otherwise they're good examples of troublesome terms. They look a lot alike, and they have similar meanings — both are found in caves, but one grows up from the ground, the other hangs down from the ceiling.

How to remember which is which? Imagine a hiker who accidentally stands in an anthill, and winds up with ants in his pants. This leads to a good memory aid: "When the mites go up, the tites come down."

Not all of the word-pairs are that easy to keep separate, but we'll give you a clear explanation of the differences, along with practical exercises to confirm your understanding.

We'll also give you a few helpful comments from some of the best current references.

Not All Authorities Agree

But remember that authorities don't always agree. Sometimes you'll find one reference saying a usage is unacceptable (or nonstandard), while another insists that it's okay.

But knowing about that lack of unanimity can be helpful.

For example, *Webster's New World Dictionary* gives *infer* as one definition of *imply*, but adds that this is sometimes considered a "loose usage." Knowing this doesn't stop you from deciding for yourself whether to use the words as synonyms. But it may help you choose a workable middle ground, such as our recommendation: keep them separate in your own speech and writing, but don't "correct" people who do otherwise.

This book is *not* intended to tell you how you should use words — nobody can or should dictate that to you. It *is* intended to tell you what some respected authorities on our language have to say about the words — about which uses are standard, which are not.

Their advice will help as you work through the exercises in this book, and the exercises will help you choose and use words with more precision and greater confidence.

One last bit of advice — don't just work with these words; play with them. Let yourself have fun while you're learning.

How To Get the Most From this Book

All the words we'll cover are commonly used — and commonly misused. Chances are that you already know the difference between some of these words — maybe most of them. But working through the book to learn any you don't know, and to refresh your memory on those you do, is worth doing.

Here are some suggestions for getting the most from this book.

1. **Work from front to back** — at least most of the time. It's okay to skip ahead to read about a pair of words you're especially interested in. But aside from that, we suggest you work through the lessons in the order they're presented here, rather than skipping around too much. One reason is that some of the exercises are cumulative — they include not only words from that lesson, but words that have been covered in the lessons before it. And occasionally, we'll even drop in a word pair that we haven't covered yet, just for fun.

2. **Use the words.** As you work through the book — and afterward — use the words as often as you can in your own speech and writing. This will confirm that you understand them, will give you good practice in using them appropriately, and will help fix them in your memory so you don't falter when you need to use them later.

3. **Practice your word-watching.** Keep an eye out for misuses in the speech and writing of others. You'll find lots in menus, newsletters, bulletins from informal organizations. And you'll also find them in the work of professional writers and editors, because they too get tangled up in these words now and then. (This doesn't mean that they're incompetent; it just means that we all need to be extra careful with these words, because if they trip up the professionals, they can trip us up as well.)

4. **Have fun with these words.** If you know someone who would enjoy working with you as you learn, you can work together, maybe challenging each other with sentences you make up. And don't embarrass anyone who confuses any of these words — that's no fun.

The Dirty Thirty

Imply-infer

We like for people to be open and straightforward in their communications with us — most of the time. But sometimes a little gentle cushioning of the truth works better.

Suppose someone you care about (a spouse, supervisor, or child) is preparing a speech, and is feeling insecure about it, maybe downright scared. You volunteer to listen to a practice run, and you see lots of things wrong with the speech. But if you blurt out a list of deficiencies, you could hurt the other person's feelings (and your relationship).

So instead of being brutally honest, you sort of bubble-wrap the truth, offering gentle hints and tactful suggestions. When you do this, you are depending on the other person to understand what you're getting at, to read between the lines.

Sure, this kind of roundabout communication takes longer, but sometimes it's essential, especially if you want to keep from damaging egos or relationships.

Both *imply* and *infer* involve this kind of communications, where the meaning is not expressed directly, but hinted at. The difference is that one of the words refers to the *expression* of ideas (speaking or writing), and the other word refers to *receiving and understanding* what's meant (listening or reading, then taking the intended hint).

So in summary, to *imply* something is to express it without saying it explicitly — to hint at it, to talk around it. You can imply with words, or by other means (a yawn may imply boredom, or sleepiness).

And to *infer* is to understand what was hinted at, to read between the lines, to "get it." Notice that inferring is a mental process, so words or gestures can not infer anything.

Mnemonic (memory aid): The middle letter of each word is a good clue. The P helps you remember that imPly is to Put meaning out there, and the F reminds us that to inFer is to get the meaning From the clues. (We often find the word *from* following close behind *infer*.)

Caution: Some good dictionaries list *imply* as one definition of *infer*, but this is often considered a loose usage.

Our advice is to keep the words separate in your own writing and speaking, but not to make a habit of correcting those who don't.

The exercise below will help make sure you can use the words in their standard senses.

Exercise: Imply — Infer

1. Do your words imply/infer that you agree?

2. May I imply/infer from your words that you agree?

3. No, I did not intend to imply/infer that; please don't draw that implication/inference.

4. The senator wouldn't give a direct answer, but he implied/inferred that he would vote for it.

5. The implication/inference I drew from her expression was that she might go along.

6. When you said that, what were you implying/inferring?

7. When you heard her say that, what did you imply/infer?

8. Your turn: Write a sentence to test knowledge of these words. _____

_____

_____

1. imply; 2. infer; 3. imply, inference; 4. implied; 5. inference; 6. implying; 7. infer

Its — It's

The slick and flashy new poster in the bookstore window caught my eye. It said that a new, unabridged dictionary had been issued by a major publishing company, and would soon be on sale there.

The dictionary, the poster said, was "The best in it's class."

Sure, it should have been *its* — without the apostrophe. Makes you wonder how such an error could sneak under the radar of all the writers, editors, and proofers who should have caught it. And this is not an isolated case — we see these two little words interchanged often, even in well edited publications.

One reason we make this mistake is that we get used to using an apostrophe to show possession — John's car, the boy's bike, the boat's engine. So when we want to say something like "The dog lost its collar," we may drop in an apostrophe, without thinking. But possessive pronouns (e.g., *hers, his, ours, theirs*) are the exception to the rule — they don't take an apostrophe.

The lesson here is that it's not enough to know the difference between these tricky word-pairs, but that we have to be constantly on guard to make sure we use the words the way we intend to.

The difference:

It's means "it is," or sometimes "it has," as in *it's easy to confuse these terms*, or *it's been a tough year*.

Its refers to something that belongs to (or is closely associated with) "it." Examples: *The dog wagged its tail,* and *The stock lost a good deal of its value.*

Mnemonic: Think of the apostrophe as an "i" printed a little above the line, so you'll look at *it's* and think "it is." Use that memory hook as you work the exercise on the next page.

Exercise: Its — It's

1. Its/it's almost noon, time to give the cat its/it's food.

2. The car has its/it's problems, but its/it's been a reliable vehicle.

3. Its/it's most worrisome fault is that its/it's hard to start on cold mornings.

4. Its/it's a mystery to me why its/it's so stubborn, but its/it's certainly true.

5. Its/it's battery has been changed, and its/it's plugs have been cleaned, but its/it's problem persists.

6. This sentence has its/it's benefits, but I'm glad its/it's the penultimate one in this exercise.

means: almost last

7. Now its/it's time for me to write an example of my own.

8. Your turn:

_____

_____

_____

i.e. — e.g.

These little abbreviations can be useful short-cuts in writing. But if you do use them, make sure you choose the one that says what you intend.

The difference:

The abbreviation i.e. (Latin for *id est*) means "that is." Use it when you want to explain, specify, or clarify (not when you want to give an example). So you'd write "My last test-grade (i.e, an *A*), made me feel good."

The abbreviation e.g. (also Latin, for *exempli gratia*) means "for example." You would use it in a sentence like "Bring any kind of dessert (e.g., cake or cookies)."

How to remember:

By taking a little liberty with the language, we can translate the i.e. as "it equals," and the e.g. as "example given."

So you'd say "Bring any kind of dessert (e.g., cookies)," because you're giving an *example* of a dessert the person might bring.

And you'd say "I hope you'll bring my favorite dessert (i.e., chocolate mousse)," because chocolate mousse *equals* your favorite dessert.

Note: The most-common way to write these abbreviations is within parentheses, with a period after each, and a comma after the second period, like this: Maybe I'll order some kind of cool drink (e.g., lemonade).

Now you can test your knowledge on the appropriate exercise (i.e., the one on the next page).

Exercise: i.e. — e.g.

1. Its/it's time for my favorite TV program (i.e./e.g., "Watch Your Words").

2. Its/it's on our only public channel (i.e./e.g., Channel 32).

3. I inferred/implied from its/it's barking that my favorite dog (i.e./e.g., Rex) was chasing something.

4. His frown implied/inferred that he didn't like my request (i.e./e.g., that I be given a week's leave with pay).

5. Its/it's true that they sell many different kinds of apples (i.e./e.g., Staymans, Granny Smiths).

6. Let's invite one of the five team members (i.e./e.g., Tom or Mark).

7. She always takes a good book (i.e./e.g., *Moby Dick, War and Peace*) on vacation.

8. He was reading from his favorite poetry book (i.e./e.g., *Talton's Verses*).

9. Your turn:

_____

_____

_____

Appraise — Apprise

The difference:

To *appraise* something is to *judge* it, to assess or estimate its value. If you apply for a mortgage loan on your house, an *appraiser* may come to look it over. During a performance *appraisal*, the supervisor evaluates the work the employee has done.

To *apprise* is to *inform*. A newscaster may promise to keep us *apprised* of any further news, or an interested person may ask to be *apprised* of any new developments.

Example of a common misuse: "Please keep me appraised." (It should be "keep me *apprised*.")

Mnemonic: Use the **i-ai** spelling difference to remember that the one with just the **i** means inform.

Also, you can think "When they *appraise* my performance, I'd like to get *praise*, or maybe even a *raise*."

Note: *Webster's New World Dictionary* agrees that they should be kept separate, and does not give either as a synonym for the other.

So keep them separate as you work the exercise on the following page.

Exercise: Appraise — Apprise

1. Please appraise/apprise the situation, and keep me appraised/apprised.

2. The car dealer will appraise/apprise my oldest car (i.e./e.g., the '67 Volvo) and appraise/apprise me of its/it's trade-in value.

3. Please appraise/apprise the applicant's qualifications, and appraise/apprise me of your rating.

4. The assessor will make an appraisal/apprisal of the value of the house, then will appraise/apprise the mortgage company.

5. The senior personnel specialist (i.e./e.g., Lee Simkins) appraised/apprised us of the results.

6. Your turn:

_____

_____

_____

1. appraise, apprised; 2. appraise, i.e., apprise, its; 3. appraise, apprise; 4. appraisal, apprise; 5. i.e., apprised

Capitol — Capital

These two words are pronounced the same, so what we have here is basically a spelling problem — one that your software won't help you with. But there's a simple way to keep them straight.

The difference:

The word *capitol* has only one common meaning — the building where the state or federal legislature meets.

Capital has several meanings. These include money or wealth (she raised capital to start her business), the city that is the seat of government, something excellent (a capital idea), an upper-case letter (a capital B), the most important (the capital reason for doing that), and punishable by death (a capital crime, capital punishment).

Example of common misuses: Washington is the nation's capitol. (It should be *capital*.)

Mnemonic: To remember the difference, make it easy on yourself by focusing on the simpler one, *capitol*. Most capitol buildings have a dome, so match the O's in dOme and capitOl. The other definitions, listed above, use *capital*.

So it's a capital idea to remember that the capitol building has a dome.

Note 1: *Capitol* is usually capitalized when referring to the building in D.C. where the U.S. legislature meets, but usually written with a small c in referring to a building where a state legislature meets.

Note 2: Some things that are near, or closely associated with, a capitol building may be spelled the same way: Capitol Hill in Washington, and businesses near the building (e.g., Capitol Cleaners, Capitol Café).

Exercise: Capitol — Capital

1. Let's drive into Virginia's capital/capitol city (i.e./e.g., Richmond) and visit the capital/capitol building.

2. I think its/it's a capital/capitol idea, if we can raise the needed capital/capitol (i.e./e.g., the money for food and gas).

3. Some businesses on Capital/Capitol Hill in D.C. use their location in their names (i.e./e.g., Congressional Cleaners).

4. She is strongly against capital/capitol punishment (i.e./e.g., executing criminals).

5. She is glad that its/it's not practiced here in the nation's capital/capitol.

6. Your turn:

_____

_____

_____

Council — Counsel

Most people pronounce these two words the same, so listening won't help us keep them straight. And because both words are legitimate, our spellcheckers won't help either.

The difference:

A *council* is a committee or group established for a specific purpose (e.g., a city council).

To *counsel* is to give advice, as in "The lawyer counseled them to pay the fee." The advice itself may be called *counsel*, as in "She gives good counsel." And the person giving the advice may be called a *counsel* (or *counselor*).

Mnemonic: To remember which is which, tie the c in counCil to the c in Committee.

Exercise: Council — Counsel

1. The lawyer was appointed council/counsel for the city council/counsel.

2. The council/counsel president said the new council/counsel gave them good council/counsel.

3. I may need to council/counsel with you before the next council/counsel meeting.

4. The personnel specialist who spoke to the management council/counsel said that a good supervisor will council/counsel new employees when needed.

5. I need your council/counsel; which word should I use?

6. Your turn:

_____

_____

_____

Cumulative Exercise

Imply/infer, Its/it's, I.e./e.g.

1. Her gesture (i.e./e.g., the one-finger salute) implied/inferred to the driver of the semi that she was displeased with its/it's maneuver.

2. May we infer/imply from his words (i.e./e.g., "No way,") that its/it's unlikely that our suggestion will be approved?

3. Don't be too quick to infer/imply from the sky that its/it's going to bring some kind of bad weather (i.e./e.g., a shower).

1. i.e., implied, its; 2. infer, it's; 3. infer, it's; e.g.

Cumulative Exercise

Appraise/apprise, Capitol/capital, Council/counsel

1. Two members of the security council/counsel are in the capitol/capital building to appraise/apprise the danger of contamination.

2. If they find anything, they should keep the mayor of the capitol/capital apprised/appraised.

3. The lawyer who's council/counsel for the council/counsel said it would be a capitol/capital idea to appraise/apprise the damage and appraise/apprise her of the findings.

Regime — Regimen

This pair causes a lot of trouble, even for some professional writers and editors. The author of a recent article in a national magazine seemed to use them interchangeably, sometimes in the same paragraph. But most dictionaries and editors make a clear distinction.

The difference:

A *regime* (ruh-ZHEEM) is a form of government, a governing group (or ruler), or the time when the ruling person/group is in power. "The dictator's regime was a brutal one," or "The king's regime lasted for seventeen years."

A *regimen* (REDGE-uh-mun) is a set of rules or practices, often rules having to do with personal discipline (e.g., health, exercise, study). "I want to make good grades, so I'm setting myself a strict regimen of study," or "To get in shape, she followed a careful regimen of exercise and nutrition."

Example of a common misuse: "Uh-oh, I've gained four pounds. I'd better get back on my health regime right away." (Should be *regimen*.)

Mnemonic: Think of the strict discipline of a military group such as a *regiment*, which sounds a lot like *regimen*.

Note: *Webster's New World Dictionary* gives as an old and "Rare" definition of *regimen* "A form of government or rule…," but that shouldn't affect the way we use the words today.

You can continue your regimen of learning more about words by doing the exercise on the next page.

Exercise: Regime — Regimen

1. The czar's regime/regimen lasted thirty years.

2. He's eighty years old, but is still going strong because of his health regime/regimen.

3. During the ayatollah's regime/regimen, he dictated a strict regime/regimen of prayer and fasting.

4. The general feared that a democratic regime/regimen would bring an end to the disciplined regime/regimen of his troops.

5. If I'm going to learn all these words, I'd better develop a regime/regimen of study.

6. Throughout the emperor's regime/regime, he kept his regiments on a strict regime/regimen of exercise and meditation.

7. I've decided that part of my vocabulary-improvement regime/regimen will be to write my own example sentences, like the following:

8. Your turn:

_____

_____

_____

1. regime; 2. regimen; 3. regime, regimen; 4. regime, regimen; 5. regimen; 6. regime, regimen; 7. regimen

Adverse — Averse

These two words look and sound a lot alike, and they have an overlap of meaning (both involve being *against* something or somebody). So they often cause trouble for good speakers and writers. But there's a fairly clear distinction between them.

The difference:

Averse is used to describe a negative mental attitude, as in "He's not averse to making more money, but he seems to be averse to hard work."

The word *adverse* describes unfavorable conditions, such as physical or climatic conditions. So you might say "We sometimes worked under adverse weather conditions," or "The miners were constantly subjected to adverse working conditions, such as foul air and dampness."

Mnemonic: The letter "d" is found in both *aDverse* and *conDitions*. This link can help you remember, because while people may be averse, they are not adverse. Only conDitions are aDverse.

So if you're not averse to a little work, test your knowledge on the following exercise.

Exercise: Adverse — Averse

1. I'm not adverse/averse to learning new words, even under adverse/averse learning situations.

2. My spouse was definitely adverse/averse to my suggestion, so I lived in an adverse/averse home atmosphere for a while.

3. He may be adverse/averse to working in such adverse/averse surroundings.

4. The adverse/averse effects of the adverse/averse desert weather began to take their toll.

5. It/it's sometimes hard to choose the right word under adverse/averse circumstances (i.e./e.g., in a high-pressure meeting).

6. The members of the swim team were adverse/averse to practicing in the adverse/averse climate.

7. I'm not adverse/averse to writing my own sentence:

_____

_____

_____

Emigrate — Immigrate

Once again we have a pair of troublesome twins that your spellchecker won't help with, and that are pronounced the same by most people. Part of the confusion is that they both have to do with more-or-less permanent moves from one place to another (usually from one country to another). But it's the *direction* of the move that sets the distinction.

The difference:

To *emigrate* is to move *out of* the country, as in "Because of the terribly adverse conditions in his homeland, he decided to *emigrate* to another country."

To *immigrate* is to *move into* a country, as in "This section of the city houses many people who have *immigrated* here from other countries."

Mnemonic: Use the first letter of each word to remind you that Immigrate means to move Into, and that to Emigrate is to Exit.

Exercise: Emigrate — Immigrate

1. She emigrated/immigrated into these United States four years ago; she'll probably emigrate/immigrate to some other country next year.

2. Under that regime's anti-emigrant/immigrant policy, nobody was allowed to leave the country.

3. But emigrants/immigrants were permitted to come (in,) because workers were needed.

4. Any newly arrived emigrant/immigrant who commits a felony will be forced to emigrate/immigrate.

5. Fleeing refugees were emigrating/immigrating from Afghanistan by the thousands; Pakistan allowed many of them (in) as emigrants/immigrants.

6. Your turn:

_____

_____

_____

1. immigrated, emigrate; 2. anti-emigrant; 3. immigrants; 4. immigrant, emigrate;
5. emigrating, immigrant

Compliment — Complement

These two are near-identical twins, with just the i-e difference. And to make matters worse, almost everyone pronounces them the same way. This means we have no problem using them in our speech, but we have to be careful in writing them. And once again, our spellcheckers refuse to help us.

The difference:

To *compliment* people is to say something nice about them. "She complimented him on his tennis serve." And the thing said is *a compliment* — "He thanked her for the nice compliment."

A *complement* is something that completes, adds to, enhances. A salesperson might say "This scarf would be a perfect complement to your outfit," or a coach might say "Lisa's skill at defense will complement the strengths of the other members of the team."

Complement is also used to mean the authorized number or size (e.g., of a group or team). "The full complement of a squadron is seven."

Mnemonic: Use the letters *i* and *e* as your keys. Remember "I like complIments," and "complEments complEte."

Exercise: Compliment — Complement

1. The newly hired onomatomaniac will be the perfect compliment/complement to our scrabble team.

2. She received a nice compliment/complement on her writing style.

3. The full compliment/complement of the team is five writers and two editors.

4. He complimented/complemented her on how her improved serve made such a nice compliment/complement to her tennis game.

5. The dessert compliments/complements the meal perfectly; my compliments/complements to the chef.

6. Your turn:

   _____

   _____

   _____

Adopt — Adapt

The difference:

To *adopt* something is to take it for your own, to assume ownership and responsibility. "Chris and Susan decided to adopt a child." Or "He'd better adopt a new attitude, or he'll be unlikely to succeed."

To *adapt* is to change to meet new or different conditions or situations. "I'd better adapt my work habits to the new job." Or "This machine part I ordered won't quite fit, but I think I can use a file to adapt it so that it will work."

Mnemonic: The middle letters will help you remember which word to use. To adOpt something is to make it your Own; to adApt something is to chAnge it.

Exercise: Adopt — Adapt

1. If you expect to adapt/adopt yourself to this team, you'd better adapt/adopt a new attitude.

2. Shall we adapt/adopt the tune for our school song as it is, or should we make a few adaptations/adoptions?

3. I didn't like working under such adverse/averse circumstances, but I managed to adapt/adopt.

4. As the coyotes emigrated/immigrated east from their western habitat, they were able to adapt/adopt to their new homes.

5. If you adapt/adopt a coyote pup, you may have to adapt/adopt yourself to a different life style.

6. My present health regime/regimen isn't working, so I guess I'll have to either adapt/adopt it to fit my new situation, or adopt/adapt an entirely new one.

7. Your turn:

_____

_____

_____

1. adapt, adopt; 2. adopt, adaptations; 3. adverse, adapt; 4. emigrated, adapt; 5. adopt, adapt; 6. regimen, adapt, adopt

Forego — Forgo

These two words are pronounced the same, and are very close in spelling. Fortunately, there's a good memory hook for keeping them separate.

The difference:

The word *forego* means "to go before," as in "Pride may forego a fall." It's often used in the *-ing* form, as in "The foregoing passage clearly tells us that...."

The slightly shorter word *forgo* means "to go without," as in "My new health regimen means that I'll have to forgo alcohol and caffeine for a while."

Mnemonic: One of these words has an *e* in the middle, the other doesn't. So follow these two good tips.

The word that means "to go beFORE" is FOREgo.

The one that means "To go *without*" is the one that *goes without the "e."*

Note: *Webster's New World Dictionary* lists *forego* as a variant spelling of *forgo*, but not the other way around. So it's a good idea to keep them separate in your own writing, while recognizing that some people use the one with the *e* in both senses.

Exercise: Forego — Forgo

1. As she concluded, the speaker said she hoped the foregoing/forgoing story would encourage us to forego/forgo smoking in the future.

2. I'm adopting a new health regime/regimen, so I'd better forego/forgo the second glass of wine.

3. A big ego is said to forego/forgo trouble, so you should forego/forgo bragging on yourself too much.

4. My budget is tight, so I'll have to forego/forgo my planned overseas vacation.

5. Clouds like those often forego/forgo a severe storm, so maybe we'd better forego/forgo our sail.

6. Your turn:

_____

_____

_____

Cumulative Exercise

Regime/regimen, Averse/adverse, Emigrate/immigrate

1. The despot's regime/regimen had such averse/adverse effects on the people that thousands attempted to emigrate/immigrate to one of the five neighboring countries (i.e./e.g., Pakistan or Uzbekistan).

2. I'm personally averse/adverse to the most extreme sentence (i.e./e.g., capital punishment), but that tyrant's regime/regimen, as shown by the starving emigrants/immigrants to my country, may cause me to reconsider.

3. We'll all have to get used to a new regime/regimen of more strict security, and will have to live under more averse/adverse conditions, unless we decide to emigrate/immigrate to some other country (i.e./e.g., Canada).

1. regime, adverse, emigrate, e.g.; 2. averse, i.e., regime, immigrants; 3. regimen, adverse, emigrate, e.g.

Cumulative Exercise

Complement/compliment, Adopt/adapt, Forego/forgo.

1. The adapted/adopted child soon adapted/adopted to the new environment, even though she had to forego/forgo the praise and compliments/complements her former classmates showered on her.

2. The foregoing/forgoing sentence is a complement/compliment to the previous exercise, which helps us adopt/adapt new words and adopt/adapt old ones for use in new ways.

3. If I want any compliments/complements on my appearance, I guess I'll have to adopt/adapt myself to an exercise regime/regimen, and forego/forgo some of the food I like best.

1. adopted, adapted, forgo, compliments; 2. foregoing, complement, adopt, adapt; 3. compliments, adapt, regimen, forgo

Affect — Effect

These two words are among the most troublesome in this book, and in our language. They're used fairly often, they're similar in spelling, and they're even closer in pronunciation. To make matters worse, each is sometimes used as a verb, and sometimes as a noun (though *affect* as a noun is uncommon). So don't feel bad if you have trouble remembering which is which. You're in good company.

The difference:

The verb *affect* has three fairly common meanings. In its most frequent usage, it means "to change or influence," as in "How will this economic downturn affect the stock market?" or "The music and poetry affected me deeply."

Another (less common) definition of the verb *affect* is "To like to have, wear, etc.," as in "When he became a professor, he affected a pipe and tweed jackets."

And a third use of *affect* as a verb is "to pretend," as in "He affected indifference to the criticism."

To *effect* (verb) something is to create it, to cause it to happen. "The medicine effected a profound change in the patient, but it did not effect a complete cure."

As a noun, *effect* means the result, or the outcome. "What effect did the medicine have?" or "The effect was unexpected."

The word *affect* as a noun is restricted almost entirely to the field of psychology, where it means something like "Emotion, emotional state, or emotional response," as in "The patient seems to have a flat affect today."

That's a lot to remember about *affect* and *effect,* so we're including the following chart to help clarify the uses, and for you to use as a handy reference if you need a refresher.

Results

	Affect	Effect
As Nouns	*Affect* is very rarely used as a noun. (In psychology, it means roughly "emotional response.")	The effect is the result. *What will be the effect?*
As Verbs	Affect begins with an "A," means "change or sway." *Will the oil spill affect the water? Will the speech affect the vote?*	Effect begins with an "E," means "to cause it to be." *The new manager effected a reorganization of the division.*

Exercise: Affect — Effect

1. How will learning these words affect/effect us? What affect/effect will it have?

2. The patient's affect/effect became brighter when he began to think he was Caesar, and he affected/effected a toga and sandals.

3. The affect/effect of his costume was ludicrous, and affected/effected the other patients adversely/aversely.

4. We should affect/effect a better way to fight terrorism; the incidents are affecting/effecting us all.

5. What affect/effect do you expect the new exercise regime/regimen to have on my health?

1. affect, effect; 2. affect, affected; 3. effect, affected, adversely; 4. effect, affecting; 5. effect, regimen

Eminent — Imminent

These two are pronounced the same and spelled differently, so we're basically dealing with a spelling problem. But it's not a tough one, because the first letters give us a good clue to the meanings.

The difference:

If something is *imminent,* it's likely to happen, and right away. "The weather forecast says a storm is imminent." So the word applies to events or such, but not to people.

The word *eminent,* however, is used for people, specifically people who are outstanding in their fields or professions. "Einstein was an eminent physicist," or "Margaret Mead was an eminent writer on the subject of different cultures."

Mnemonic: "HE or shE is Eminent; It is Imminent." Or on a broader scale, remember that **pEople** are Eminent, but thIngs are Imminent.

Exercise: Eminent — Imminent

1. She's an eminent/imminent journalist; they're predicting that a Pulitzer prize for her is eminent/imminent.

2. If an operation is eminent/imminent, I hope there's an eminent/imminent surgeon on the staff.

3. The eminent/imminent weather forecaster said that a storm appeared eminent/imminent.

4. Even an eminent/imminent linguist like him can mix these words up.

5. She's eminent/imminent; it's/its eminent/imminent.

6. Your turn:

_____

_____

_____

Flaunt — Flout

These words are used just often enough so that we should know the difference, but not quite often enough to make it easy to remember that difference.

The difference:

To *flaunt* something is to make a <u>showy</u> or <u>brazen display of</u> it, as in "Big Jim liked to flaunt his diamond rings under everybody's nose," or "Sylvia loved to flaunt her voluptuous body."

To *flout* is to <u>openly ignore</u>. The word is most often used in regard to rules or laws, as in "The police are using cameras to catch drivers who flout the speed limit," or "He flouted the no-smoking rule by lighting up wherever he wanted to."

Mnemonic: The *aunt* at the end of *flaunt* helps us remember that the shapely Auntie Mame flaunted her physical beauty. And you can tie the *out* at the end of *flout* to what the smoker who flouted the rule should do with his cigarette, or where he should take it.

Note: *Webster's New World Dictionary* lists "flout" as one definition of "flaunt," confusing the issue even more. But because so many careful writers keep these words strictly separated, you should do the same — just don't argue with those who do otherwise.

Exercise: Flaunt — Flout

1. Don't flaunt/<u>flout</u> this rule: Learn lots of new words, but try not to <u>flaunt</u>/flout your knowledge.

2. She slipped into her bikini and said "If you've got it, <u>flaunt</u>/flout it."

3. He liked to <u>flaunt</u>/flout his muscles, flaunting/<u>flouting</u> the normal standards of modesty.

4. He enjoyed flaunting/<u>flouting</u> the rules; he'd often <u>flaunt</u>/flout a huge cigar right under the "no smoking" sign.

5. If you flaunt/<u>flout</u> the law, you may find a policeman <u>flaunting</u>/flouting his badge in your face.

6. Your turn:

_____

_____

_____

1. flout, flaunt; 2. flaunt; 3. flaunt, flouting; 4. flouting, flaunt; 5. flout, flaunting

Ingenious — Ingenuous

The difference:

This is an unbalanced pair, because one of them seems to be used a lot more often than the other. Maybe that's because most people are nice, as the one that means "really smart, exceedingly clever" is the one most-often used. That word is *ingenious,* of course, and it's considered a real compliment (and a complement to your vocabulary).

The other one is not exactly an insult, but it's not flattering either. To say that someone is *ingenuous* is to say that the person is innocent by nature, free of guile, incapable of deceit. That's nice, but there's also a slight suggestion that the ingenuous person is naïve, and some dictionaries give *naïve* as one definition of the word. A stock character in some plays is the *ingenue* (ahn-zha-noo), an artless and simple young girl.

Mnemonic: The pronunciation is a giveaway. The complimentary word is pronounced "in-genius," and that *genius* pretty well says it.

So now it's easy to remember that the other one (pronounced in-GIN-you-us) is not a genius at all.

Exercise: Ingenious — Ingenuous

1. He's so ingenious/ingenuous that he'll believe anything.

2. If his idea works, it's ingenious/ingenuous; if it doesn't, he's ingenious/ingenuous.

3. Einstein had some ingenious/ingenuous ideas, but his early teachers considered him unsophisticated, perhaps even ingenious/ingenuous.

4. An ingenious/ingenuous con artist will always find some way to rook ingenious/ingenuous people.

5. Goldie's open smile may look ingenious/ingenuous, but behind that face lies an ingenious/ingenuous mind.

6. Your turn:

_____

_____

_____

1. ingenuous; 2. ingenious, ingenuous; 3. ingenious, ingenuous; 4. ingenious, ingenuous; 5. ingenuous, ingenious

Ordinance — Ordnance

These two are not used nearly as often as some of the others, like *it's* and *its*, and this infrequency can make it hard to remember which is which. The good news is that the words themselves contain a built-in clue.

The Difference:

An *ordinance* is a local law or regulation, most often a *city ordinance* (enacted by a city council).

Ordnance is military weaponry. The word is usually applied to cannons or artillery, but sometimes to other things (e.g., vehicles, ammunition).

Mnemonic: This one's fairly easy. The only difference in the spelling of the two words is that little *i* that's in one but not the other, so you can remember *cIty ordInance*, with an *I* in each word. Or if you prefer, you can focus on the one without the *i*, and think "*I* stay away from ordnance."

u

Exercise: Ordinance — Ordnance

1. The town council passed an ordinance/ordnance against keeping ordinance/ordnance within the municipal limits.

2. In the army, he was assigned to an ordinance/ordnance unit.

3. We're a country of laws, not guns, so let's use an ordinance/ordnance instead of ordinance/ordnance.

4. As we walked around Burke Lake, we could hear the ordinance/ordnance from Fort Belvoir.

5. He's a Luddite; he thinks there should be an ordinance/ordnance against new industry.

6. Your turn:

_____

_____

_____

1. ordinance, ordnance; 2. ordnance; 3. ordinance, ordnance; 4. ordnance; 5. ordinance

Simple — Simplistic

The difference:

Simple is a neutral term. By itself, it doesn't imply either goodness or badness. A simple idea may be very good, even ingenious. (The term can be unflattering, though. Referring to someone as *simple* suggests that the person is *ingenuous,* or worse.)

But *simplistic* is almost invariably negative, because the word means "too simple, unrealistically oversimplified, naive." So if someone offers a simplistic solution, that person probably doesn't understand the problem. A person who does this repeatedly could also be called a *simplistic*, which one of my dictionaries defines as "Someone given to simplistic explanations, theories, etc."

For some reason (maybe through love of the long word), many people use *simplistic* when they mean *simple* — thus choosing a word that's almost opposite what they intended. Of course words change over time, and if enough people adopt this definition, we'll have to go along with them. But for now, it's best to keep them separate — for simplicity's sake.

Exercise: Simple — Simplistic

1. Her idea was simple/simplistic, but it worked just fine.

2. His idea sounded simple/simplistic to me, so I was skeptical.

3. Some people wrongly assume that a person who uses simple/simplistic, everyday words has simple/simplistic ideas.

4. Telling teenagers "Just say no" sounds like a simple/simplistic approach to the drug problem.

5. The other suggestions were too simple/simplistic, but his was simple/simplistic and effective.

6. Your turn:

_____

_____

_____

1. simple; 2. simplistic; 3. simple, simplistic; 4. simplistic; 5. simplistic, simple

Cumulative Exercise

Affect/effect, Eminent/imminent, Flout/flaunt

1. The fact that he's an eminent/imminent onomatomaniac has no affect/effect on me; he shouldn't flout/flaunt his vocabulary that way.

2. He flouted/flaunted the "No talking" rule by demanding to know if learning all the new words would affect/effect his reputation, or if a salary increase would be eminent/imminent.

3. She affected/effected a Scottish accent, flouting/flaunting her knowledge of the Highlands, and pretended to be an eminent/imminent authority on the history of the British Isles.

Cumulative Exercise

Ingenious/ingenuous, Ordinance/ordnance, Simple/simplistic.

1. Thinking he knew more than he did, the ingenious/ingenuous young recruit gave a simple/simplistic description of the ordinance/ordnance used in the battle.

2. Her idea is workable and ingenious/ingenuous; its/it's simple/simplistic and inexpensive, requiring only that the council/counsel pass a city ordinance/ordnance.

3. Only a very ingenious/ingenuous person would think that we could eliminate terrorism by passing a few ordinances/ordnances; that's far too simple/simplistic.

Stationary — Stationery

Because most people pronounce these words the same way, what we have here is another spelling problem. Not a serious problem though, because there's a near-foolproof way to remember which is which.

The difference:

To say that something is *stationary* means that it doesn't move, that it stays put.

The word *stationery* refers to the paper (including envelopes) we use for writing and sending letters.

These two are often interchanged, usually by writing *stationary* when we mean *stationery*. More than once I've seen a store sign, hanging above writing paper and envelopes, that directed customers to "Stationary."

Mnemonic: Because one is spelled with an *a*, the other with an *e*, we can use that little difference to remember that the one with the **A** means to stA*y*, and the one with the **E** is what we write l**E**tt**E**rs on. (Or if you prefer, think of **E**nvelope.)

Exercise: Stationary — Stationery

1. The post-office building is stationary/stationery, but its/it's contents are stationary/stationery.

2. You'll find envelopes in the stationary/stationery section of the store.

3. Is your computer portable or stationary/stationery?

4. He received a missive on scented stationary/stationery.

5. Now that his military unit is stationary/stationery, he can find more time to use his stationary/stationery.

6. Your turn:

_____

_____

_____

Principle — Principal

One of these words (*principal*) has several common definitions, while the other is pretty much restricted to a single common meaning. So as with *capitol-capital*, let's focus on the simpler one.

The difference:

Although *principle* has at least a half-dozen definitions, here's the one that's used more often than all the others combined: "A *principle* is a guiding *rule.*" (There's a built-in memory aid here — notice they both *principle* and *rule* end in *le*).

An example of this usage: "The principle we follow is to keep things simple without getting simplistic."

A related definition, "integrity," is probably second in frequency of usage, as in "She's a person of principle."

The word *principal* has several definitions in common use. It may mean most important (the principal reason for improving one's vocabulary), the amount of a debt or investment (the payment includes principal and interest), someone authorized to conduct business (a meeting of principals only), or the chief executive of a school (the students hope the principal is their pal).

Mnemonic: Focus on the simpler word *principle*, and remember the *-le* ending of *rule*. Once you've got that down, it's easy to associate the "-al" ending of *principal* with the other definitions. If you need more memory help, you can mentally connect the "-al" ending with "all," as in "all the other definitions are likely to take the "-al" spelling.

Exercise: Principle — Principal

1. It's/its not the principle/principal (morality) of the thing; it's/it's the principle/principal (money).

2. The pauper may be a man of principle/principal, but the banker is a man of principle/principal.

3. The principle/principal rule some people live by is "Spend the interest, but don't touch the principle/principal."

4. The high-school principle/principal had trouble keeping his faculties about him.

5. We have several rules to live by, but our principle/principal principle/principal is this quote from Xavier Onassis: "Always look out for number one."

6. Your turn:

_____

_____

_____

1. it's, principle; it's, principal; 2. principle, principal; 3. principal, principal; 4. principal; 5. principal, principle

There — Their — They're

Instead of tricky twins, in this case we have troublesome triplets. Although some people make a clear distinction in pronouncing these words, most of us sort of lump them together phonically, pronouncing them almost the same way. That makes it easy to use them in conversation, but harder to remember which is which in our writing.

The difference is clear enough though, and we do need to keep them separated.

The Difference:

There has two common meanings. One is *in (or at or to) that place*, as in "It is there," or "Do you go there often?" The other use is to state existence, as in "There are lots of rabbits on Coney Island," or "There is good reason to learn these words."

Their means *belonging to them*, as in "It's their house."

They're means *they are*, as in "They're not at home just now."

Exercise: There — Their — They're

1. You say they want to know where t _new_ English
   books are? T _neve_ they are;
   t _hey've_ right t _there_ .

2. And t _their_ other books are
   t _neve_ too.

3. T _hey're_ always asking where
   t _heir_ books are.

4. Tell the terrorists, wherever t _hey're_ hiding, that
   we will go t _here_ and find them.

5. T _hey're_ wrong if they think we won't;
   t _heir_ plans will never succeed.

6. Your turn:

   _____

   _____

   _____

Two — To — Too

Another triple-threat here, all three pronounced the same, but with entirely different meanings. Most of us know what these words mean, but it's easy to get careless and let the wrong one slip into our writing (and we'll get no help from our spellcheckers).

The Difference:

Two is a number.

To is used as a preposition (to class, to the pub), or as part of an infinitive (to study, to learn).

Too means *also* or *excessively* (I'll come too, if that's not too many).

How to remember:

For the number, think of *two twins*.

For the preposition, think of *to to*wn. To remember the infinitive, think of *to remember*.

For the last one, *too*, think of *adding another "o."* The "added" gives a clue to the meaning of "additional, excessive."

Exercise: Two — To — Too

1. If both you t_wo_ are going t_o_ the play, I'd like to go t_oo_.

2. T_oo_ many cooks spoil our plans t_o_ enjoy good soup.

3. Tw_o_'s company; three's way t_oo_ many.

4. Please ask someone else t_o_ work on these t_wo_ sentences, t_oo_.

5. There are t_oo_ many sentences t_o_ complete in t_wo_ minutes.

6. Your turn:

_____

_____

_____

Your — You're

We don't have any good stats on this, but our experience tells us that mistakes with this pair are more likely to result from being rushed or tired or just careless, rather than from ignorance. So train yourself to mentally raise a yellow flag before you write either one of them, and to take the few seconds needed to make sure you write it right.

The Difference:

Your means "belonging to you." (So does *yours*, incidentally, and notice that it doesn't take an apostrophe.)

The contraction *you're* means "you are."

How to Remember

Before writing either one of these words, stop and remind yourself that the apostrophe is a signal that something has been left out. This will help you think of the expanded form: *you are*. And if *you are* is what *you are* intending to communicate, then *you're* right in choosing the one with the apostrophe.

Exercise: Your — You're

1. If y _ou've_ sure you know the word to use, write y _our_ answer in the blank.

2. Maybe y _our_ mama says y _ou're_ wonderful, but y _ou're_ not.

3. But I'll agree with y _our_ claim that y _ou're_ a very good wordsmith.

4. Y _our_ work on these exercises indicates that y _ou're_ really getting better.

5. Okay, now y _ou're_ on y _our_ own.

6. Your turn:

Criterion — Criteria

The Difference

There's a simple difference in the meanings of these two words: one's singular, one's plural. But for some reason, the plural form (*criteria*) is used much more often than the singular form (*criterion*). That's probably the reason so many people say or write things like "The only criteria we use is cost." It should be "The only criterion...."

Mnemonic: Notice that the singular form ends in -*on*. Mentally tacking on an "e" will give you *one*, which should be enough to remind you that the word is singular.

Exercise: Criterion — Criteria

1. The ice-skaters were judged by three criteria/criterion.

2. There's only one criteria/criterion for membership: enough money to pay the dues.

3. How many criteria/criterion do they use in appraising show horses?

4. The single most important criteria/criterion for evaluating an applicant is a good vocabulary.

5. I don't think one criteria/criterion is enough; we should have at least three criteria/criterion.

6. Your turn:

_____

_____

_____

Cumulative Exercise

Stationary/stationery, Principle/principal, They're/their/there

1. According to the letterhead on they're/their stationary/stationery, they're/there both principles/principals in the partnership.

2. The sailors said their/they're guiding principal/principle was to keep the telescope stationary/stationery while the ship rolled.

3. The gurus said their/there principal/principle guidebook was the Turza, because the principles/principals they live by are written they're/their/there.

Cumulative Exercise

To/two/too, Your/you're, Criterion/criteria.

1. Your/you're to/two/too new to understand all the criterion/criteria we're judged by.

2. There are several, but the two/too principle/principal criterion/criteria are quality of you're/your work and how your/you're apprised/appraised by you're/your supervisor.

3. All to/too often, your/you're apt to find vague criterion/criteria in performance ratings.

1. you're, too, criteria; 2. two, principal, criteria, your, you're, appraised, your; 3. too, you're, criteria

Compulsion — Compunction

We don't use either of these words all that often, and maybe that's part of the trouble. They don't occur often enough for us to become really familiar with them, but they do show up in the language just often enough so that we need to know the difference.

The Difference

In its most common use, a *compulsion* is a mental urge (often irrational) that's too strong to resist. "She felt a compulsion to shoplift, even though she had plenty of money."

The term *compunction* means a feeling of slight regret for something done, a pin-prick of conscience. The word is often used with *no*, to show the absence of such regret, as in "The judge said she had no compunction at all for handing down the maximum sentence to the drug dealer."

How to Remember

For *compulsion*, you can think of *compel*, which means "to force." A compulsion, then, forces a person to do something, even if it's irrational.

The word *compunction* is also related to a word that will help you remember its meaning. The word is *puncture*, which suggests a pin-prick of conscience. The kind you might feel if you didn't do the next exercise.

Exercise: Compulsion — Compunction

1. The country feels a strong compulsion/compunction to bring the terrorists to justice.

2. Most people would feel absolutely no compulsion/compunction about punishing them.

3. The mother felt a twinge of compulsion/compunction after disciplining her child.

4. In the novel *Compulsion/Compunction*, one man felt an irresistible urge to get revenge on another.

5. He committed the act with no compulsion/compunction whatsoever, and slept well afterward.

6. Your turn:

_____

_____

_____

1. compulsion, 2. compunction, 3. compunction, 4. Compulsion, 5. compunction

Mitigate — Militate

These two seem to have a fairly low usage rate, but when they do show up in our language, they can cause trouble.

The Difference

To *militate* against something is to make it less likely to happen, as in "His record of traffic violations will militate against his being hired as a chauffeur." The word can be used in a positive sense, as in "Her excellent performance ratings will militate in favor of her being hired." It can be, but for some reason it rarely is. In a very high percentage of uses, the negative form prevails, so the word *militate* is often followed by *against*.

To *mitigate*, on the other hand, almost always has a positive flavor to it. It means "To soften, to make less harsh, etc." For example, "The defendant was found guilty, but his previously clean record will probably mitigate his sentence."

How to Remember

The spelling of *militate* suggests *military*, which in turn suggests something that "fights against," the way cutting class will fight against getting good grades.

On the other hand, you have *a mitten* — soft, comfy, making life easier — pretty close to what *mitigate* means.

Exercise: Mitigate — Militate

1. He applied for the security job, but his police record will militate/mitigate against him.

2. However, his good behavior in prison may militate/mitigate his chances.

3. Worry about the economy may militate/mitigate against consumer spending.

4. But an economic upturn could have a militating/mitigating effect/affect.

5. Her lack of writing experience may militate/mitigate against her getting the journalist's job, but her excellent vocabulary may militate/mitigate that weakness in her background.

6. Your turn:

_____

_____

_____

1. militate, 2. mitigate; 3. militate; 4. mitigating, effect; 5. militate, mitigate

Home in on — Hone in on

A fairly common problem with these two words is that many people say "hone in on," when the phrase that's acceptable as standard English is "home in on." Members of the military often use "home in on" to mean "guide (as by radar, laser, heat) to a target or destination."

To *hone* is to sharpen, and the fine-grained stone used to sharpen blades is also called a hone (or a whetstone).

This substitution of *hone* for *home* occurs even among intelligent, well educated speakers and writers. (Maybe they've been doing it all their lives, as one respected professor with a PhD in linguistics told me he had.) But once the problem is called to their attention, such people are unlikely to repeat the substitution. Instead, they'll home in on the right word.

Mnemonic: Home in on the military use, and think of guiding something to its intended *home*. And to hone your skills, home in on the right answers in the next exercise.

Exercise: Home — Hone

1. If you want to avoid confusing your readers and listeners, you should hone/home in on word-pairs you're/your not sure about.

2. That way you can home/hone your/you're verbal skills.

3. Too many people say "home/hone in on" when they should say "home/hone in on."

4. To hone/home means to sharpen, as with a stone; to hone/home in on something means to focus or concentrate on it.

5. So we've honed/homed in on some tricky words, and now you're/your homing/honing your/you're skill in using them accurately.

Cumulative Exercise

Compulsion/compunction, Militate/mitigate, Home/hone.

1. The new editor's compulsion/compunction to home/hone in on insignificant errors will militate/mitigate against her acceptance by her peers.

2. Her supervisor felt no compulsion/compunction about warning her of this, hoping the editor would home/hone her people skills, and that this would militate/mitigate the writers' resentment.

3. In dealing with tricky words, you can militate/mitigate against errors by developing a compulsion/compunction to home/hone in on those words that give you the most trouble (i.e./e.g., your own verbal *betes noires*).

To Whom, or Not to Whom?

Of all the words in the English language, *whom* is surely one of the most troublesome.

For one thing, it's not always easy (and sometimes downright hard) to decide whether to use *whom* or *who*. In a sentence like "Give it to *who(m)ever* asks for it," where the word comes right after a preposition (*to* in this case), it sort of "feels like" we should use the *whom* form. We shouldn't. *Whoever* is the word we want (because it's the subject of the verb *asks*).

For another thing, many people dislike the word *whom*, and think those who use it are pretentious — especially those who find ways to work it into their language when they could easily use other words, or simply leave it out.

You choose whether or not to use it, and how often. But if you do use it (or if you edit other people's writing), you should know when to use *whom* (instead of plain old *who*).

Here are two answers to the question of how to deal with the troublesome term — a short one, and a long one.

The longer one first. To decide whether the pronoun form should be *who* or *whom*, use this three-step process. 1) Find each verb in the sentence. 2) Find the subject of each verb. 3) Use *who* (or *whoever*) as subject of a verb. (*Whom* and *whomever* are used as objects.)

Here's a real sentence, patterned after one from a major newspaper, for you to practice on.

> *The suspect, whom a witness said was apparently intoxicated, is now in police custody.*

There are three verbs in the sentence: *said, was,* and *is*. To find the subject of the first, ask "Who said?" The witness said, so that's the subject. Repeat with the other verbs, and you get the *suspect* is in custody, and *whom* was intoxicated.

So the newspaper goofed — it should be *who*.

they = who
he = who

him = whom
them = whom

Now for the short answer: Don't use *whom*. Revise the sentence. Write your way around it. Use *whom* only when you have to, which is almost never. And when you're talking, don't worry about grammar rules, just say *who* or *whoever*. If anybody asks why you think it's okay to do that, tell them you read it in a book.

Note: Although it doesn't come up often, the *who* form is also used as the predicate nominative, as in "It was who?"

Exercise: To Whom, or Not to Whom?

Note: As you do this exercise, see if you find any sentences where *whom* is grammatically correct, but simply leaving it out would improve the sentence.

1. Give the check to/ whomever/whoever asks for it.

2. A bartender must learn to hide his contempt for the people/ whom/who he serves.

3. Who/whom do you think is responsible?

4. Send the bill to/ whomever/whoever the accountants say is responsible.

5. The person who/whom they think has the gold rules.

6. I'm meeting some friends who/whom I haven't seen in a long time.

7. Who/whom do you think should be arrested in the price-fixing mess?

8. They should arrest whomever/whoever they find has profited illegally.

9. She is the person who/whom they believe knows all the answers to this exercise.

10. I would like to meet whomever/whoever really does know all the answers.

Note: We could improve sentences 2 and 6 by simply leaving *whom* out.
10. whoever
1. whoever, 2. whom, 3. who, 4. whoever, 5. who, 6. whom, 7. who, 8. whoever, 9. who,

Advise — Advice

Both these words have to do with making suggestions or giving information, especially when you're telling others what you think they should or should not do.

The difference is that one (a verb) refers to the *act of telling,* while the other (a noun) means what is told — the *suggestions or information given.*

So when you *advise* someone, you're giving that person *advice.*

You can use the S in adviSe as a clue to remembering the difference. If you tie it to the S in Say, it will help you remember that adviSe (like Say) is a verb.

Exercise: Advise — Advice

1. I'm a little confused about these two words; can you advice/advise me as to the difference?

2. Thank you for your advice/advise; I'm sure it'll be helpful.

3. One job of the Senate is to advice/advise and consent.

4. However, the president doesn't always appreciate the advice/advise given.

5. He is always quick to advice/advise others about what they should do, but his advice/advise is often wrong.

6. That means his listeners are ill-adviced/advised; they should seek advice/advise elsewhere.

7. Anne gives advice/advise to whoever/whomever asks her to advice/advise them.

Could/Couldn't Care Less

Okay, you might ask, which of these two expressions is wrong, and which is right?

It's not quite that simple. The fact is that each can be okay in certain situations, but that lots of people use one when they mean the other.

The expression "I couldn't care less" means "I don't care at all — my level of caring is at zero, so it couldn't be lower." No problem so far, because the words and the meaning are clear, and are in agreement. But for some reason (maybe because it's easier), people often say "I could care less" to mean the same thing — that they don't care at all.

Suppose your friend has been jilted by a former girlfriend, and you ask if he's hurt. "Nah," he scoffs, "She can do whatever she wants — I could care less." His meaning may be clear, but his words literally mean the opposite.

To make it even worse, some careful users of the language do use "I could care less" in its literal sense — meaning "I do care." Suppose a different friend lost a job, or a spouse, or a contract, and you ask how the friend is taking it. "Well," your friend says ruefully, "I could care less." That means your friend does care, maybe a great deal.

So don't get careless with *care less*.

Exercise: Could/Couldn't Care Less

1. I'm not worried about this quiz — I could/couldn't care less.

2. Alas, I lost my job for misusing words. How am I taking it? Well, I could/couldn't care less.

3. The expression "I could/couldn't care less" literally means "I really do care — maybe a lot."

4. But "I could/couldn't care less" literally means "I don't care at all."

5. My friends waste a lot of time watching soaps on TV, but for myself, I could/couldn't care less about those silly programs.

6. I'm not exactly heartbroken by the dear-John letter, but I'll admit I could/couldn't care less.

7. He should be worried about the final exam, but he acts as if he could/couldn't care less.

1. couldn't; 2. could; 3. could; 4. couldn't; 5. couldn't; 6. could; 7. couldn't

Cumulative Exercise

Who/whom, Advise/advice, Could/couldn't care less

1, We should reward whoever/whomever answers all these items correctly.

2. Will you advise/advice me on this exercise?

3. Sure. I'll give advice/advise to whoever/whomever asks for it.

4. Who/whom do you think will ask you? And who/whom would you ask?

5. I could/couldn't care less about how much money he makes.

6. I would advice/advise whoever/whomever wants to talk "correct" to learn these words.

7. Is he one of those people who/whom hiring official reject because of grammar errors?

8. I'm afraid so; they advise/advice him to apply to whoever/whomever might hire him.

9. That would be whoever/whomever could/couldn't care less about employees' language.

10. He's sorry he didn't take my advice/advise; he admits that he could/couldn't care less.

Lagniappe

Congratulations. You've worked your way through the entire list of more than thirty dirty words and pairs and triplets. As a reward, here are a couple more for *lagniappe*. (That word — pronounced *lan-YAP* — means a little something extra given to a customer or friend, something like a sucker given to a child by a barber.)

Bimonthly and Twelve p.m.

No, these two aren't likely to be interchanged, like the other word-pairs we've looked at. They're grouped together because they're troublesome, and because they both have to do with time.

Bimonthly

I've asked several adult classes this question: "If you subscribe to a magazine that's published *bimonthly*, how many issues will you receive each year?"

About two-thirds say six, one-third say twenty-four.

So what's the right answer? You could say either, neither, or both. Most people use the word to mean "every two months" (which it usually means in magazine publishing).

Webster's New World Dictionary lists both definitions, noting that "twice a month" is now rare.

But if lots of people still use it to mean "twice a month," we have a potential problem.

So what should we do? The first step is to recognize that this is not an either-or question. If we assume one has to be wrong, and the other right, we're falling into the old false-dichotomy trap, which is common in language. Instead of trying to decide which of two answers (or words or punctuation marks or sentence structures) is the "right" one, we need to look for other possibilities.

And there's an easy one here. Why not just avoid using *bimonthly*, and instead say "every two months" or "twice a month." If we do that, the problem goes away.

Twelve p.m.

What's the problem here? Again, it's potential misunderstanding.

The Latin *post meridiem* means "after noon," and is used to designate the time between twelve noon and twelve midnight. But twelve p.m. can't be between them (i.e., between twelve and twelve), so it has to be one of them. Which?

The context will usually make it clear, as in "We'll meet for lunch at twelve p.m.," or "We didn't get out of the late-night movie until twelve p.m." But what about "The deadline for filing your application is twelve p.m.," or "The satellite will pass overhead at twelve p.m."?

There's enough uncertainty involved to make us wary, and again there's a simple solution: avoid it when there's any possibility of misunderstanding (or maybe just avoid it, period). Instead, say "noon" or "midnight."

Note: The word *noon* gives us a good example of how words change. It comes from the Latin word for *ninth*, and originally meant "the ninth hour." By the Roman method in use then, hours were counted from sunrise, so this would have put noon at about three in the afternoon. Still later the word was sometimes used to mean "midnight" (e.g., Shakespeare's phrase "the very noon of night").

Just Between You and I

Look at these sentences:

> *They invited my wife and I over for coffee.*
>
> *The supervisor wanted Rebecca and he to attend the meeting.*
>
> *Just between you and I, pronoun misuse is a common problem.*

The bad news, as they say, is that all these sentences use the wrong pronoun form, and that it's a common mistake. We hear and read sentences like these often, because even good writers and speakers sometimes get tangled up in their syntax.

The good news is that in almost all sentences like these, there's a quick and easy fix. First, notice that the troublesome pronouns in these sentences don't stand alone — each one is paired with another word, usually a noun. If you're not sure which pronoun form to use, simply repeat the sentence, *leaving the other word out,* and you'll get your answer.

For example, repeating the first sentence this way gives us: *They invited I over for coffee.* We'd never say that, so it's immediately clear that *me* is the form we want. Same with the next one — we wouldn't say *wanted he to attend.* The word *between* makes the last example a little trickier, but *between you and me* is the form to use.

So when you have a pronoun paired with another word, and you're not sure if you have the right form, remember this rule: *When in doubt, leave it out.* Leave the other word out long enough to see which form of the pronoun to use, then put it back in.

Try that on the following exercise, and you'll see how well it works.

Exercise: Just Between You and I...or Is it Me?

1. The editor asked Jan and I/me to proofread these sentences.

2. For heaven's sake, don't mention this to Chris and she/her.

3. Between Con and I/me, we had just enough money.

4. From the expression on his face, we suspected that he was talking about she/her and I/me.

5. Such behavior is beneath the dignity of people like Terry and I/me.

6. Why don't you give the job to he/him and I/me to do?

7. She invited Richard to go to the seminar with Charlotte and she/her.

8. Just between you and I/me, this is a pretty good rule.

Also Available from LandaBooks

Read excerpts and purchase online at www.landabooks.com.

The Landa List: Grammar Guidelines, Proofreading Practices, Punctuation Principles

You've heard of the "ninety-ten" principle — that ninety percent of the work (or mistakes, or problems) usually comes from ten percent of the people.

The Landa List applies that principle to rules about writing and speaking. It sorts out the most important rules, and gives concise, easy-to-read explanations and examples. This handy reference isn't intended to replace exhaustive style manuals such as *Chicago* or *APA*, but it will answer most of your everyday writing questions. More than 95 percent, in our experience.

In addition to grammar and punctuation rules, it lists 100 of the most-frequently misspelled words, and gives you proofreading marks (with useful hints). And it includes, in condensed reference form, almost all the dirty-thirty words you've worked with in this book.

ISBN: 1-57420-001-1 $5.95

The Writing Process: A Step-by-Step Approach for Everyday Writers

Writing is more than a way to record sentences we've already shaped in our heads. As someone famously said, that's just typing. This book will help you develop an approach that includes the thinking part of writing. A series of logical steps will lead you from idea (or assignment) to finished written work.

It answers some basic questions that every writer faces: How do I get organized? What do I do first? What next? How do I evaluate my drafts? How about word choice? When have I said enough? How should I end?

Designed to help almost any writer, *The Writing Process* is also an excellent tool for teachers of writing, as well as for parents who want to give their youngsters an extra boost.

ISBN: 0-9729920-2-2 $11.95

Words Clusters: Build A Vocabulary That Works for You

Successful people have good vocabularies. You've heard it before, and you'll hear it again.

But having a good vocabulary means more than knowing lots of words — it means being able to choose and use the word that says exactly what you mean. It means knowing the subtle (and not so subtle) differences between words. A laconic remark is different from a cryptic one. Being frugal isn't the same as being stingy. A republic isn't a democracy.

One of the best ways to improve word-choice skills is to learn groups of words that are related to a core topic, but that differ in some important ways. This book leads you through many important word clusters, including forms of government, attitudes toward other people, approaches to money, and more.

In *Word Clusters*, you'll find words you'll actually use, practical exercises that reflect choices you'll make in your work and professional life, and — perhaps just as important — you'll have fun.

ISBN: 0-9729920-4-9 $11.95

Your Notes

Printed in the United States
106236LV00002B/1-30/A

9 780972 992053